Mel Bay Presents

CHILDREN TIN WHISTLE METHOD

By
Mizzy McCaskill & Dona Gilliam

MW00583001

Contents

ONLINE AUDIO

To Access the Online Audio Go To:
www.melbay.com/95305BCDEB

Musical Facts

Staff

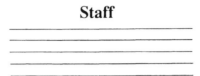

The **staff** consists of the 5 lines and 4 spaces upon which notes are placed.

Treble Clef

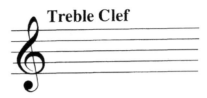

The **treble clef** or **G clef** is placed at the beginning of a staff. It indicates the pitch of the notes to follow because it circles the G line.

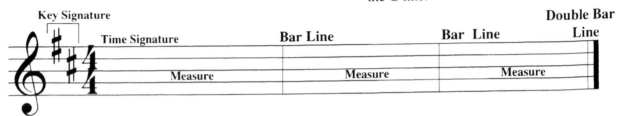

Bar lines are used to divide the staff into measures. The space between bar lines is called a **measure.** The **double bar line** is used at the end of a musical selection.

Key Signature for D

This book is written for a tin whistle that is pitched in D (when all of the tone holes are covered the note D sounds). The key of D has two sharps (#) noted in the key signature-F sharp and C sharp. Although the whistle is pitched in D it can be played in other keys.

Time Signature

4 3 2   Top number tells how many counts in a measure.

4 4 4   Bottom number tells what kind of a note receives one count (1/4 or one quarter note).

Note Names

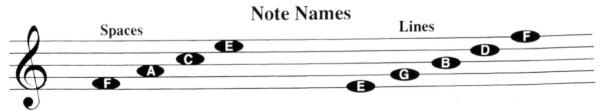

Note and Rest Values

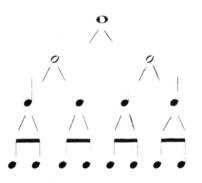

whole note = whole rest

half notes = half rests

quarter notes = quarter rests

eighth notes = eighth rests

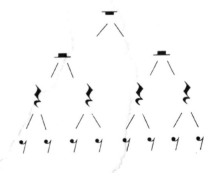

Playing Position

To Hold:

Cover the top three tone holes with the first three fingers of the left hand. Cover the bottom three tone holes with the first three fingers of the right hand.

To Sound:

Sit up straight. Place the mouthpiece between the lips. Instrument rests on thumbs. When possible adjust thumbrest to feel comfortable. Take a normal breath, and move tongue as if saying ' too' while blowing a steady stream of air.

Fingering Chart

● closed hole

○ open hole

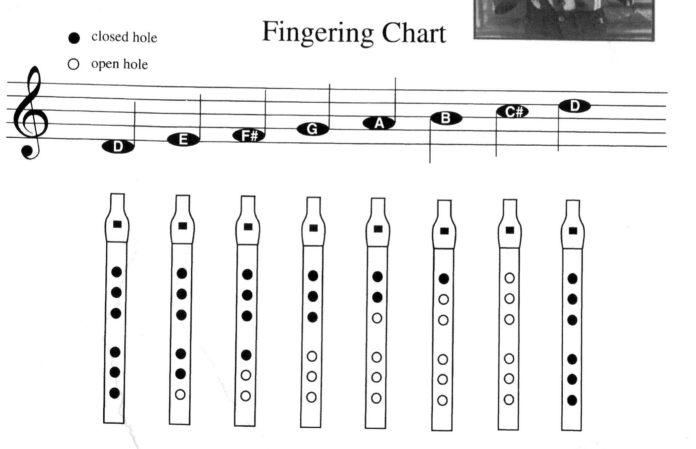

3

First Notes B, A, and G

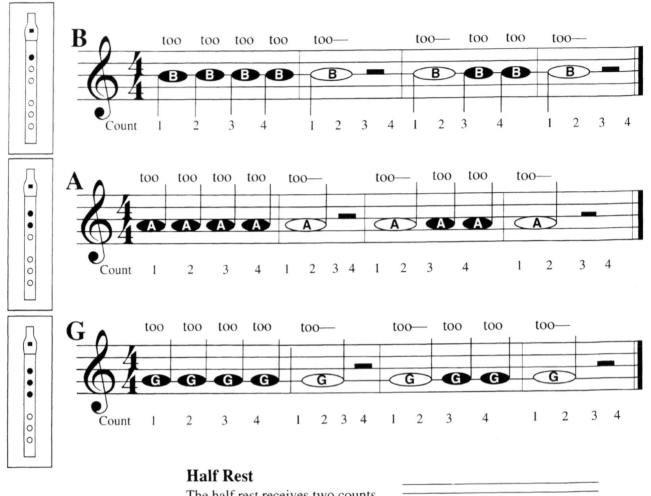

Half Rest
The half rest receives two counts.
Notice that it sits on the line.

Merrily We Roll Along

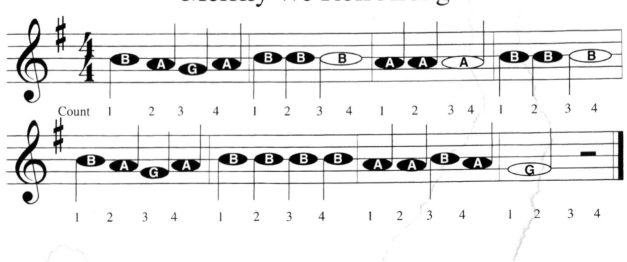

Hot Cross Buns

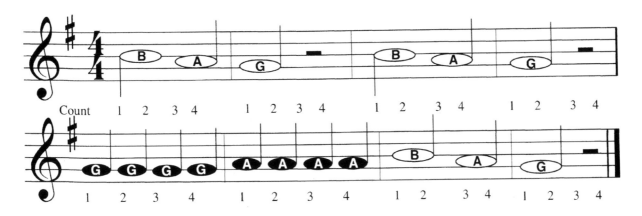

Repeat Signs

Repeat signs indicate that music between the two signs is to be repeated. If only one repeat sign is used return to the beginning.

Au Clair de la Lune

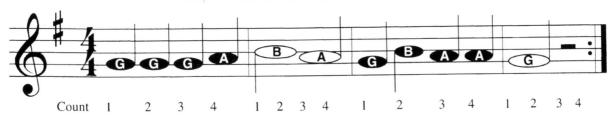

Quarter Rest

The quarter rest receives one count.

Fais Do Do

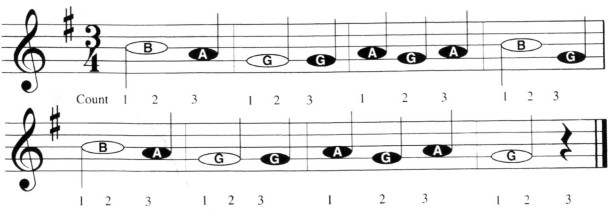

New Note C Sharp (C#)

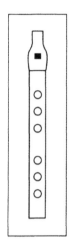

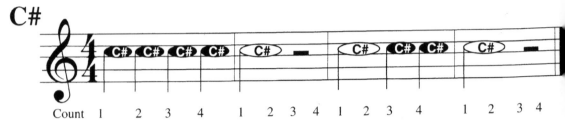

Note Review

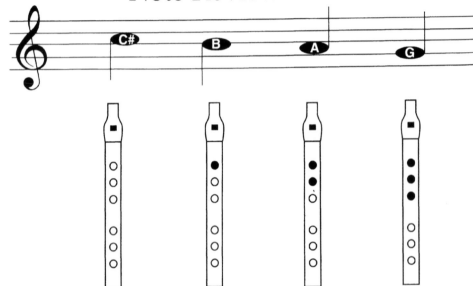

Merrily We Roll Along

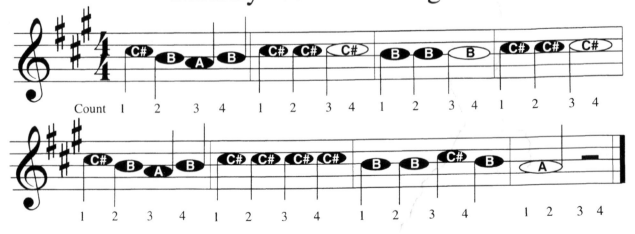

Au Clair de la Lune

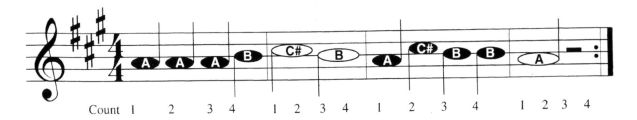

Count 1   2   3   4   1   2   3   4   1   2   3   4   1   2   3   4

Hot Cross Buns

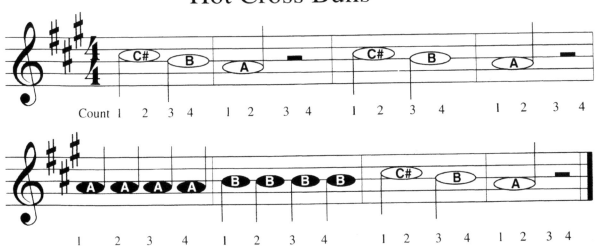

Count 1   2   3   4   1   2   3   4   1   2   3   4   1   2   3   4

1   2   3   4   1   2   3   4   1   2   3   4   1   2   3   4

Fais Do Do

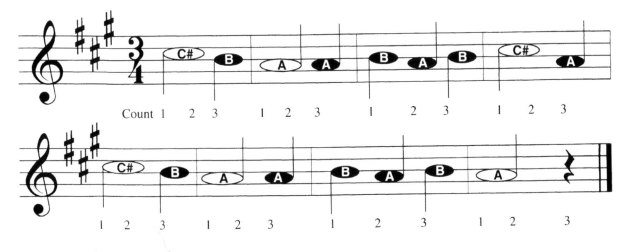

Count 1   2   3   1   2   3   1   2   3   1   2   3

1   2   3   1   2   3   1   2   3   1   2   3

Taped Tone Holes

The use of transparent tape can assist the beginner in learning to play the lowest notes on the tin whistle. Tape is used to cover the tone holes and to help establish correct pitch and playing position. Players who are able to control all tones with ease may choose not to use the tape. If the tape is not used, follow the open (o) or closed (•) fingerings as given.

Tape the top 3 tone holes. Make sure the tape seals all three holes.

Place fingers **1**, **2**, and **3** of the left hand on the top three tone holes (over the transparent tape).

Place fingers **4**, **5**, and **6** of the right hand on the bottom three tone holes.

Whole Rest
The whole rest receives four counts. Notice that it hangs from the line.

Lowest Notes F#, E, and D

F#

Count 1 2 3 4   1 2 3 4   1 2 3 4   1 2 3 4

E

Count 1 2 3 4   1 2 3 4   1 2 3 4   1 2 3 4

D

Count 1 2 3 4   1 2 3 4   1 2 3 4   1 2 3 4

8

Merrily We Roll Along

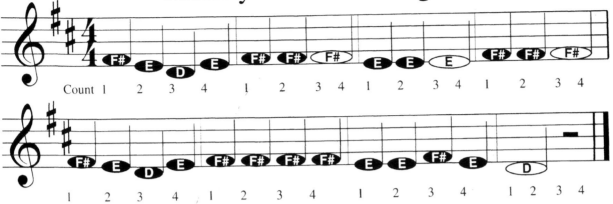

Hot Cross Buns

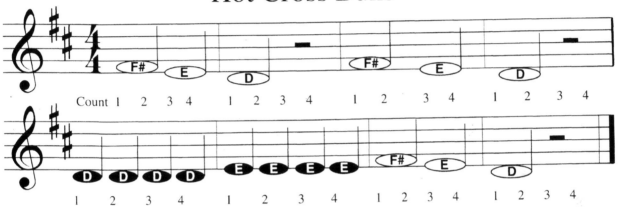

Fais Do Do

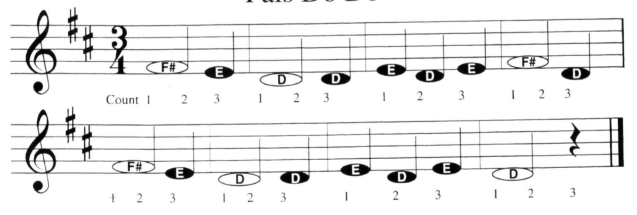

Au Clair de la Lune

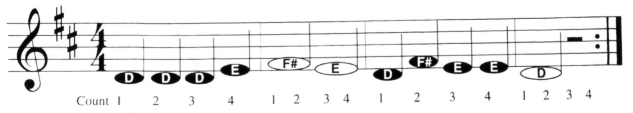

9

Low D

Blow **softly**.
Play a **low** note.

How long can you hold **Low D**?
Count the seconds.

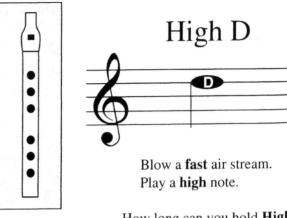

High D

Blow a **fast** air stream.
Play a **high** note.

How long can you hold **High D**?
Count the seconds.

Points to Remember:

1. Tongue the beginning of each note as if saying *too*.
2. Blow a slow, steady air stream.
3. Should moisture form in the mouthpiece and prevent notes from sounding, remove moisture by placing finger over the opening in the mouthpiece and blowing hard.

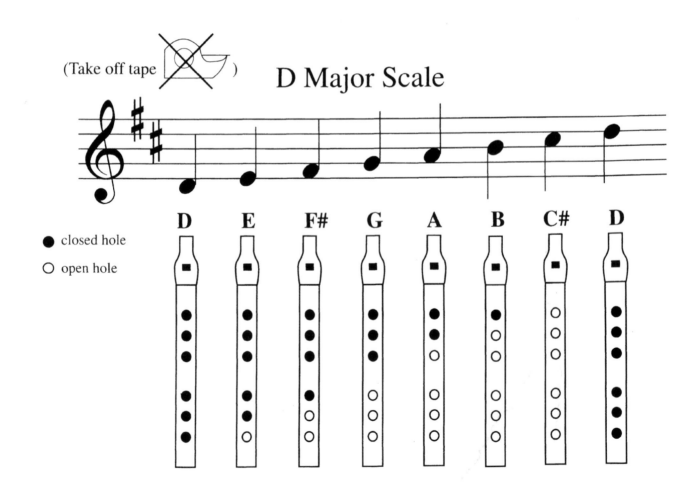

(Take off tape)

D Major Scale

● closed hole
○ open hole

D E F# G A B C# D

C is an abbreviation for Common time, which is another name for $\frac{4}{4}$ time.

' A **breath mark** indicates the proper place to breathe when playing.

Tin Whistle Scale Song

I have a tin whis - tle I play it eve - ry

day. Friends come from miles a - round

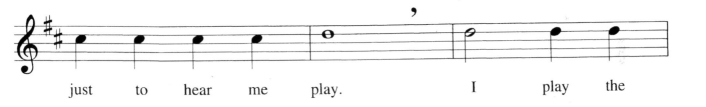

just to hear me play. I play the

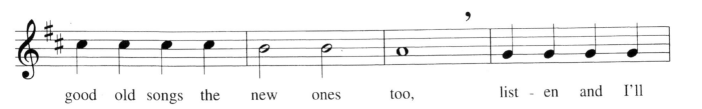

good old songs the new ones too, list - en and I'll

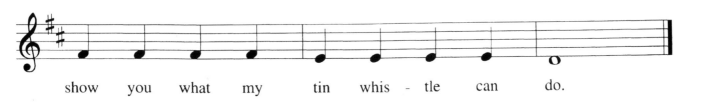

show you what my tin whis - tle can do.

11

A **round** is a piece in which two or more players begin at different times in the music. In the following rounds, each player begins when the previous player reaches the number 2.

Mason's Round

Morning Awaketh (Round)

Scotland's Burning (Round)

Go Tell Aunt Rhody

D. C. al Fine is an abbreviation for **Da Capo al Fine.**

D. C. al Fine tells the player to repeat from the beginning and play until the **Fine** marking.

Au Clair de la Lune

Fine

D. C. al Fine

Dotted Half Note

Tie

Count   1   2   3

A **tie** is a curved line connecting two notes of the same pitch. They are played as one note.

Dotted Half Note

Count   1   2   3

The **dot** is equal to one half the value of the note it follows. In this example ♩ + ♩ = ♩ ·

Eliza Jane

14

Oats, Peas, Beans

Lazy Mary

Three Blind Mice (Round)

The following piece begins on the last count of a measure. This note is called a **pick-up note.** When a piece begins with one or more pick-up notes the last measure of the piece will be shortened by the value of the pick-up note(s).

My Hat It Has Three Corners

For He's A Jolly Good Fellow

Eighth Notes

The eighth note receives one half of a count and is written with one flag or connecting bar.

Use the quarter note beat when counting eighth notes, and divide each beat into its equal parts.

Over in the Meadow

Old MacDonald

Hole in the Bucket

Bile Them Cabbage Down

Frères Jacques (Round)

This Old Man

Hey Lolly, Lolly

Bury Me Out On The Prairie

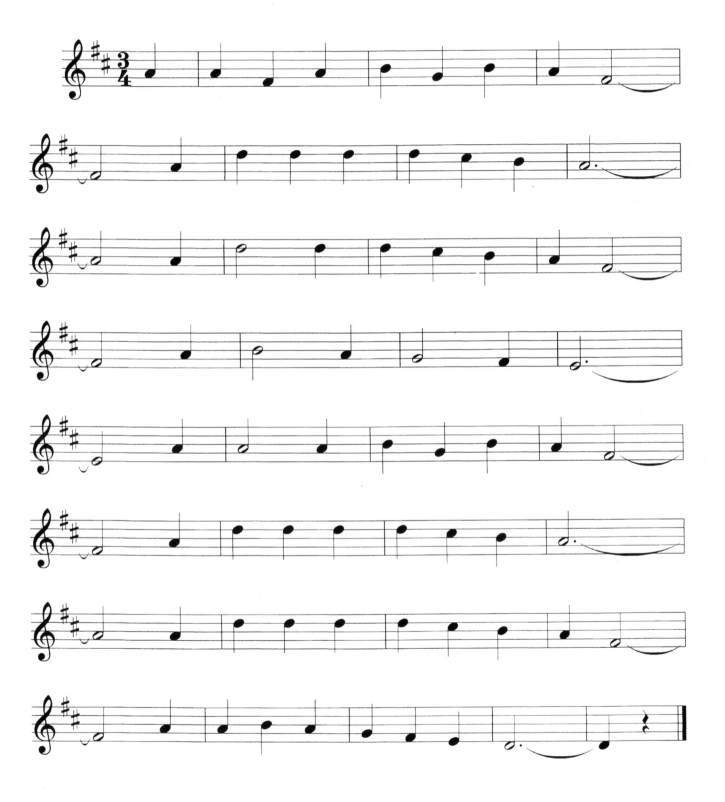

New Note C Natural

When the key signature (shown at the beginning of each staff line) does not show C♯, the player must use C natural (C) throughout the piece. Many of the following pieces use C natural. Check the key signature before playing to see whether or not you will need to use the C natural fingering.

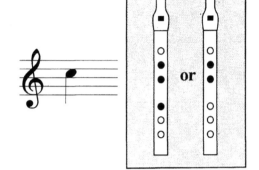

Polly Wolly Doodle

Down at the Station (Round)

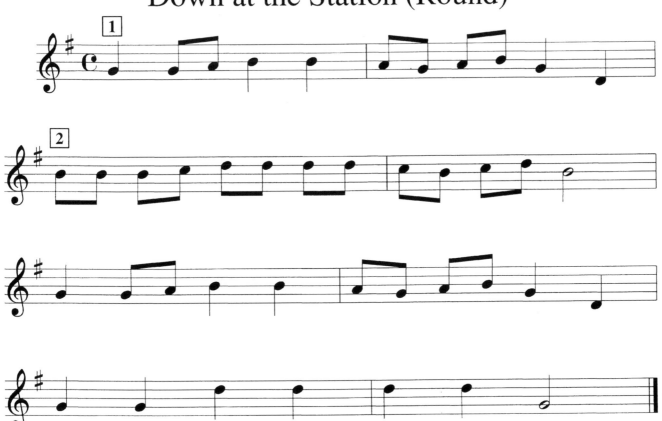

Sur Le Pont, d'Avignon

Fine

D. C. al Fine

Bingo

Dotted Quarter Notes

played in same rhythm

The Muffin Man

Home on the Range

The Wheels on the Bus

Baa, Baa, Black Sheep

Oh, Susanna

A **fermata** ⌢ is the symbol for a 'pause.' Notes with a fermata marking are often held longer than their usual value. On the accompanimental cassette, the notes beneath each fermata continue for one additional measure.

Man on the Flying Trapeze

31

Extended Fingering Chart

Made in the USA
Middletown, DE
08 September 2018